Original title:

Shared Lullabies

Author: Sebastian Sarapuu

ISBN HARDBACK: 978-1-80560-037-4

ISBN PAPERBACK: 978-1-80560-502-7

Bedtime Ballads

The stars twinkle bright,
As the moon whispers soft,
Crickets sing their tune,
In the cool night loft.

Children's dreams take flight,
On pillows, they rest their heads,
While shadows dance lightly,
In the quiet, they tread.

The clock ticks away time,
Each second a lullaby,
Wrapped in warmth and love,
As night draws nigh.

Under blankets so snug,
With stories in the air,
Whispers of adventure,
Recreate a world rare.

Soon daylight will break,
But for now, sleep's embrace,
In this tender moment,
Find your peaceful place.

Together in Slumber

Two hearts beating softly,
In the glow of the night,
Dreams intertwine gently,
Wrapped in love's delight.

Whispers fill the silence,
With promises so sweet,
Side by side in stillness,
Where time and love meet.

Stars keep watch above,
Casting dreams from afar,
In the realm of slumber,
Together we are.

The rhythm of our breaths,
A lullaby of peace,
As we drift together,
In this sweet release.

Beneath the same blanket,
With hands tightly clasped,
We journey through the night,
In dreams, we are grasped.

Soft Echoes of Love

In the hush of the night,
I hear your heartbeat's song,
A melody so gentle,
Where we both belong.

Moonlight spills like silver,
On dreams that softly flow,
Whispers of sweet comfort,
In the night's warm glow.

Every sigh a secret,
Every smile a grace,
In this sacred silence,
We find our embrace.

Time drifts like a feather,
In the calm of our space,
Echoes of love linger,
In the night's soft embrace.

Before dawn's first light,
Let's cherish this bliss,
In the depths of slumber,
Find the joy in this.

Night's Embrace

The world fades away,
As darkness takes its hold,
In night's gentle arms,
We let our dreams unfold.

Shadows waltz together,
In the moon's pale kiss,
A tapestry of stars,
Woven into bliss.

With every whispered word,
We drift into the deep,
In all that is silent,
Our hearts choose to leap.

Crickets serenade us,
With their soothing tune,
As we float in slumber,
Beneath the watching moon.

Night wraps us in comfort,
A blanket of pure peace,
In this beautiful moment,
Let our worries cease.

Chords of Dusk

As the sun dips low, the shadows play,
Whispers of night, chasing light away.
Colors blend softly, the sky's warm hue,
In this quiet hour, the world feels new.

Songs of the evening, gentle and sweet,
Crickets begin to join, a rhythmic beat.
Each note a reminder of fleeting time,
In the chords of dusk, life's subtle rhyme.

Echoing Hopes in Harmony

In a world of dreams, where wishes float,
Hearts sing together, a hopeful note.
Voices rise high, like birds in flight,
Chasing the stars that twinkle bright.

Melodies linger, in shadows they weave,
Carrying stories that we dare believe.
With every echo, a promise made,
In harmony's embrace, our fears will fade.

Twilight's Embrace

The sky transforms, a canvas wide,
Under twilight's wings, we run and hide.
Stars ignite slowly, a sparkling team,
Guiding our hearts in a tender dream.

Softly the night calls, a gentle lure,
Whispers of secrets, mysterious and pure.
In the calm of dusk, worries dissolve,
In twilight's embrace, we find resolve.

Nostalgic Night Songs

Beneath the moon's glow, memories swell,
Each shadow a story, each whisper a spell.
Candlelight flickers, shadows dance near,
Singing the songs of a yesteryear.

Time drifts like smoke, through open air,
Cherished moments hung like dreams to share.
In the still of night, our laughter rings,
Nostalgic night songs, the heart still sings.

Cradle Songs of Silence

In the hush of the night,
Gentle whispers flow,
Soft as stars that twinkle,
In the cradle below.

Shadows dance on walls,
Cradling dreams so sweet,
While the world is paused,
In this tender seat.

Fingers weave a lullaby,
With the breeze's sigh,
Carried on the wings,
Of a nightbird's cry.

Sleep now, little one,
Close your weary eyes,
The moon watches over,
Under velvet skies.

Tomorrow brings the sun,
With its golden rays,
But for now, dear child,
In silence, stay.

Melodies Under the Moon

Beneath the silver glow,
Of a moonlit night,
Stars hum ancient tunes,
In soft, gentle light.

Crickets join the song,
With a rhythmic cheer,
While the world drifts away,
All worries disappear.

The breeze carries whispers,
Through the dancing trees,
Melodies entwined,
In the rustling leaves.

Hearts beat in sync,
With the night's embrace,
Together we find peace,
In this sacred space.

So let's sway gently,
In the soft night's song,
Under the watchful moon,
Where we belong.

Dreams We Sing Together

In the twilight's glow,
Our voices blend as one,
Chasing distant stars,
Until the night is done.

With every breath we take,
We paint the skies anew,
A symphony of hope,
In shades of vibrant hues.

Hand in hand we wander,
Through shadows and light,
On paths woven softly,
As day turns to night.

Dreams flutter like butterflies,
In the garden of our hearts,
Each note a petal dancing,
As our journey starts.

Let's sing of tomorrow,
With every whispered plea,
Together we'll create,
Our own harmony.

Echoes of Dusk

When the sun dips low,
And the sky wears gray,
Echoes of soft whispers,
Begin to softly play.

The horizon blushes,
In colors warm and deep,
As dusk wraps the world,
In a quilt of sleep.

Birds call to each other,
In a farewell tune,
While the stars prepare,
To welcome the moon.

Gentle shadows lengthen,
As the night unfolds,
Carrying the secrets,
That the darkness holds.

So breathe in the dusk,
Let your worries slide,
In the echoes of twilight,
Let peace be your guide.

Twilight's Tender Touch

The sun dips low in the sky,
Colors blend, a soft goodbye.
Whispers of night begin to dance,
In shadows deep, dreams take a chance.

Stars emerge with gentle grace,
Each twinkle holds a secret place.
The moonlight spills, a silver glow,
Guiding hearts where love can grow.

In the hush, the world slows down,
Nature dons her evening gown.
Night's embrace, a tender shroud,
In twilight's arms, we feel so proud.

Crickets sing their lullabies,
Underneath the velvet skies.
Breathless moments, soft and sweet,
In this stillness, our souls meet.

As darkness wraps the fading light,
We find solace in the night.
In twilight's grasp, we find our way,
Together lost, till break of day.

A Lull Before Dawn

The night is deep, a quiet hush,
In dreams we wander, feel the rush.
Each heartbeat slows, a peaceful sigh,
Awaiting light that soon will rise.

The stars are dimming, one by one,
As shades of night are gently spun.
In this stillness, calm takes hold,
Stories whispered, yet untold.

Beneath the weight of velvet skies,
Hope lingers softly, never dies.
With every breath, a promise made,
In morning's arms, we won't be swayed.

The moon gazes with knowing eyes,
As time unravels, darkness flies.
In dreams, we find the strength to stay,
Awake with love, to greet the day.

So let this lull wrap round your heart,
Each moment savored, a work of art.
Before dawn breaks with golden crowns,
Embrace the night, and wear your brown gowns.

Embracing the Silence

In the quiet, whispers bloom,
Bathed in light, dispelling gloom.
Gentle moments, softly spun,
Feel the peace, a race well run.

The world outside begins to fade,
In stillness, shadows start to braid.
Time stands still, ticks slow down,
We find joy in the calm, profound.

Nature breathes in muted tones,
A sanctuary away from stones.
Hearts entwined in wordless grace,
In this silence, we find our place.

Stars align with gentle care,
In the quiet, love lays bare.
Each silence speaks, a sacred space,
Where dreams and hopes together trace.

Embrace the stillness, feel the glow,
In heartbeats shared, the love will flow.
Together in this cherished night,
We hold each other, until light.

The Melody of Our Spirits

In harmony, our hearts entwine,
A dance of souls, pure and divine.
Every note, a story told,
In melodies both warm and bold.

The world fades with each subtle sound,
In our music, magic is found.
Reviving dreams in whispered tunes,
Beneath the gaze of watchful moons.

Together we blend, soft and free,
Creating a symphony, just you and me.
With every rhythm, our spirits soar,
In the cadence of love, we find more.

Resounding echoes through the night,
Guided by stars, we feel the light.
A chorus of dreams encircling wide,
In this melody, we'll always abide.

Our hearts, a canvas, colors bright,
Painting the silence with pure delight.
In the dance of time, we'll forever stay,
In the melody of our spirits, come what may.

Whispering Through the Night

Stars twinkle softly in the sky,
Gentle winds carry a sigh.
Shadows dance on the ground,
In the hush, secrets are found.

Crickets sing their lullabies,
Moonlight glimmers, never lies.
Branches sway with a breeze,
Nature hums with such ease.

Thoughts wander like clouds above,
Wrapped in a blanket of love.
Dreams take flight in the gloom,
Wrapped in the night's soft bloom.

Silhouettes merge with the dark,
Every heart finds its spark.
Invisible threads pull tight,
Whispering through the night.

With every breath, night grows deep,
Promises in silence keep.
Resting under the starry light,
Lost in the whispering night.

Conversations with the Moon

Underneath the silver glow,
Whispers of the night bestow.
Dreams take shape in soft reply,
Conversations with the sky.

Stars unveil their stories bright,
As shadows deepen in the night.
Sculpting thoughts with every beam,
The moon listens as I dream.

Mirrors glow to sea and land,
Guiding with a gentle hand.
Take a breath in hope's embrace,
Heartbeats dance in this space.

Casting light upon the sea,
The moon reveals what's meant to be.
In the silence, truths arise,
Unfolding right before our eyes.

Floating thoughts on a midnight stream,
Sharing wishes, heart's sweet dream.
The night unfolds its tender tune,
In conversations with the moon.

Nurtured in Darkness

In the cradle of the night,
Shadows weave a soft delight.
Whispers linger, secrets grow,
Nurtured where few dare to go.

Wrapped in velvet, worlds collide,
Fear takes flight, dreams abide.
Stars above twinkle with grace,
Embracing each hidden space.

Roots stretch deep within the earth,
Silent journeys, quiet birth.
In the dark, foundations lay,
Nurtured in the night's array.

Gathered close in twilight's thrall,
Eager hearts begin to call.
Life emerges strong and free,
Nurtured by night's certainty.

With every shadow, stories thrive,
In darkness, we are alive.
A gentle sigh, a quiet tune,
Nurtured by the watchful moon.

The Coziness of Nightfall

As daylight fades, the world grows calm,
Wrapped in night's embracing balm.
Stars appear, a welcoming sight,
In the coziness of night.

Blankets pulled, the shadows play,
Softly losing light of day.
Candles flicker with warm glow,
Setting hearts in gentle flow.

Crickets chirp, a soothing choir,
Nature's hush ignites the fire.
Whispers float on evening's breeze,
Stirring dreams with such ease.

Beneath the quilt of navy blue,
Thoughts drift softly to what's true.
In the stillness, hearts ignite,
Finding peace in the night's light.

With each heartbeat, time does weave,
Stories waiting to believe.
Snuggled close, all feels just right,
In the coziness of night.

Echoes of Comfort

In the hush of night, whispers play,
Gentle memories drift, softly sway.
Hearts find solace in the serene glow,
Wrapped in warmth, where tender love flows.

Laughter lingers in the faded light,
Echoing stories that feel just right.
Every sigh a balm to weary souls,
Together we mend, as comfort unfolds.

Shadows dance on the walls we share,
Embracing silence with a soothing air.
In these moments, peace intertwines,
A sacred bond that forever shines.

Through the window, starlight gleams,
Cradling us softly in fragile dreams.
As echoes fade, a promise remains,
In comfort's embrace, love never wanes.

From the depths, sweet echoes rise,
Whispering solace under vast skies.
Hearts entwined, we'll brave the night,
In each other's arms, we find our light.

Melodies of Togetherness

Through the ages, our song will soar,
Harmonies linger, forevermore.
In every note, a story unfolds,
Together we wear hope like gold.

Hands entwined, we sway with the breeze,
Moments shared bring hearts to ease.
In the rhythm, our spirits align,
Creating a world where stars brightly shine.

With every laugh, a chord is played,
In the tapestry of love, we're not afraid.
Voices rise, a sweet refrain,
In the music, we find joy not in vain.

As colors blend in twilight's embrace,
Together, we carve out a sacred space.
Every heartbeat, a pulse to remember,
In the warmth of love, our hearts are tender.

Songs of the past echo in our dreams,
In melodies woven with gentle themes.
Together we sing, through joy and through strife,
In every note, we celebrate life.

Softly Singed Horizons

As dawn breaks, colors gently bloom,
Filling the air, dispelling the gloom.
Softly singed, the horizon ignites,
Welcoming dreams in shimmering lights.

Waves kiss shores with a tender sigh,
Painting the sky with hues that fly.
In the distance, adventures call,
Filling our hearts with hopes that enthrall.

Breathe in deep, the morning's embrace,
A canvas awaiting our bold trace.
With every step, new paths we find,
Chasing the sun, leaving fears behind.

Gentle whispers dance through the trees,
Carrying secrets on the waking breeze.
In nature's choir, we find our song,
Beneath the horizon, where we belong.

Softly singed by the dawn's delight,
We journey onward, hearts aflame bright.
Embracing the promise of the new day,
In every sunrise, we find our way.

Beneath a Blanket of Sound

Nightfall hushes the bustling streets,
Cocooned in whispers, our heartbeats meet.
Beneath the stars, we find our place,
Wrapped in a melody, a warm embrace.

The world fades as we sway to the tune,
Moonlight dances, casting shadows so soon.
Every note binds us in a gentle sway,
In this symphony, we linger and play.

Raindrops tap on windows, a soft refrain,
A lullaby soothing, washing away pain.
With every breath, music fills our souls,
Weaving our dreams as the night unfolds.

In this refuge, the chaos subsides,
Lost in the rhythm, where love abides.
Beneath the blanket, we quietly sound,
In each other's arms, peace is profound.

So let the night serenade our hearts,
In timeless echoes, where magic starts.
Together we find, as stars gently surround,
A world transformed beneath a blanket of sound.

Synchronized Dreams

In the quiet of night, we soar,
Two souls dancing, seeking more.
Whispers of hope in the air,
Together we dream without a care.

Stars align in a cosmic embrace,
Guiding our hearts to a tranquil place.
Fleeting moments, time drifts slow,
In synchronized dreams, our love will grow.

Each heartbeat echoes in the dark,
A rhythm born of a timeless spark.
With every breath, our spirits meld,
In this realm, our fears are quelled.

Through skies of velvet, we glide,
Hand in hand, with nothing to hide.
The tapestry of dreams unfolds,
In vivid hues, our story told.

As dawn approaches, we take flight,
Leaving traces of our starlit night.
In the daylight, memories gleam,
Forever bound in synchronized dream.

Hushed Notes in the Stillness

In the quiet dusk, a song begins,
Hushed notes linger, where the light thins.
Each sound a whisper, soft and low,
In the stillness, emotions flow.

The trees sway gently, a rhythmic sway,
Nature's chorus at the end of the day.
Echoes of love weave through the air,
In hushed notes, we find solace there.

Crickets serenade the twilight sky,
As stars appear to silently sigh.
Moments suspended, time fades away,
In the cool night, our hearts play.

Breezes carry secrets, sweet and light,
Tender melodies etched in the night.
Under the moon, we softly tread,
In hushed notes, our souls are fed.

Here in this realm, we lose all fears,
Bonded in music, the world disappears.
A symphony woven, a sacred trust,
In the stillness, it's more than just dust.

The Language of Moonlight

Glowing softly, the moon takes flight,
Casting shadows in the velvet night.
A silver whisper, secrets unfold,
In the language of moonlight, stories told.

Stars conspire in their distant dance,
Inviting dreams to take a chance.
With every glow, a pathway shines,
Illuminating our tangled lines.

The world transformed under her gaze,
In the stillness, we drift through a haze.
Words unspoken, hearts intertwine,
In the moon's glow, everything aligns.

Echoes of laughter, a timeless sound,
In the embrace of night, we are found.
Softly woven, like silk and lace,
In the language of moonlight, we find our place.

As dawn creeps in, her light will fade,
Yet in our hearts, the night won't trade.
For every moment, a treasure, unplanned,
In the language of moonlight, hand in hand.

Soothing Shadows

In twilight's embrace, shadows grow,
Gentle whispers, secrets to know.
A calming breath, the day retreats,
In soothing shadows, time gently meets.

Trees dance lightly, casting a spell,
Soft rustles of leaves, a tranquil swell.
Every silhouette tells a tale,
In the hush of dusk, we softly exhale.

Moonlight drapes a silken sheet,
Inviting solace, a rhythmic beat.
Together we wander, lost in grace,
In soothing shadows, we find our place.

With every step, the world quiets down,
Nature's lullaby replaces the sound.
Hearts unwind in the fading light,
In the soothing shadows, everything's right.

As stars emerge in their twilight glow,
We linger still where the soft winds blow.
In the night's cradle, we gently sway,
In soothing shadows, forever stay.

Heartfelt Melodies at Dusk

Soft whispers fill the evening air,
As colors dance, beyond compare.
The sun dips low, a gentle sigh,
While dreams take flight in twilight sky.

In shadows deep, our hearts entwine,
With every note, a love divine.
The stars awake, they start to glow,
As secrets shared, begin to flow.

A serenade beneath the trees,
Where laughter mingles with the breeze.
In every glance, a story told,
Of moments cherished, hearts consoled.

With every chord, emotions rise,
Reflecting all that never lies.
As dusk envelops, we find our pace,
In heartfelt melodies, we embrace.

The world fades out, it's just us two,
In harmony, our love shines through.
Together here, as night unfolds,
We weave our tale, a song of souls.

The Night That Sees Us

In the hush of night, we find our place,
Under the moon's soft, silken grace.
Whispers of shadows gently play,
As stars above guide our lost way.

Every heartbeat echoes through time,
A silent pulse, a gentle rhyme.
The sky unveils its deep embrace,
While dreams awaken without haste.

Together here, beneath the vast,
We share our truths, our shadows cast.
The night, a witness to our sighs,
A tapestry of whispered lies.

In every glance, a promise shines,
Unspoken words, our love defines.
Under the watchful, twinkling light,
We become one, lost in the night.

So here we stand, hand in hand tight,
The night wraps us in its delight.
In every moment, love intercedes,
The night that sees us, the night that leads.

Weightless Voices

In the air, our laughter sways,
Weightless voices, bright displays.
Echoes of joy that dance around,
In every note, our love is found.

Floating softly, like the breeze,
Carrying dreams with gentle ease.
Together we sing, in perfect stride,
With every heartbeat, side by side.

Through the night, under the glow,
Our songs entwine, the world below.
In harmony, we rise and dive,
A melody where souls survive.

Every whisper, a treasure shared,
Weightless dreams, forever bared.
Through the silence, let us soar,
In each note, we find much more.

So let us sing, till dawn appears,
Carving moments, banishing fears.
In every sound, our spirits trace,
Weightless voices, a warm embrace.

Singing Under the Stars

Under a canopy of shining light,
We gather close, hearts shining bright.
The world falls silent, time stands still,
As melodies flow, a gentle thrill.

With every chord, magic starts,
A symphony binding our hearts.
The stars above seem to align,
In perfect rhythm, your hand in mine.

Soft as whispers, our voices blend,
In the night, where joys ascend.
The universe listens, drawing near,
Each note a promise, crystal clear.

As songs of old echo through space,
We find our dreams in this sacred place.
With every strum, the night ignites,
A tapestry of our shared delights.

In the cool night air, our spirits soar,
Singing under stars, forevermore.
Together we weave, a tale so true,
In every heartbeat, I sing for you.

Folding Into Dreams

In twilight's calm embrace, we glide,
To realms where shadows dance and hide.
With whispered hopes, our spirits soar,
Folding softly to dream's sweet shore.

Beneath the stars in velvet night,
We chase the dawn with hearts alight.
Each breath a thread, each pulse a rhyme,
As echoes weave the fabric of time.

A gentle hush, the world spins round,
In slumber's grasp, pure peace is found.
With every sigh, we drift away,
To where the heart's true wishes play.

In dreams where wishes bloom and thrive,
The soul awakens, feels alive.
With every fold, a story spins,
A tapestry where love begins.

Voices Wrapped in Harmony

In twilight's glow, soft murmurs rise,
Like whispers shared beneath the skies.
Each note a thread, each word a chord,
Voices blend, a sweet accord.

Together we weave a song so bright,
A symphony that dances in light.
Melodies twirl through the starlit air,
Binding our hearts with tender care.

Echoes ripple, like waves on sand,
Resonate deep, as hand meets hand.
In the quiet, our spirits sing,
A chorus born on love's soft wing.

Voices cradle the night's embrace,
In every breath, a thrilling space.
Harmonies flow, a river's stream,
Together we bask in sweet daydream.

The Night's Gentle Breath

The night exhales in whispers low,
A lullaby that starts to flow.
Stars blink softly, just for me,
In this moment, I am free.

Cool winds carry stories old,
Secrets of the moon, untold.
With each sigh, the darkness hums,
In the stillness, magic comes.

Crickets play their symphony,
Nature's voice in harmony.
As shadows stretch and shadows fall,
I feel the pull, the night's soft call.

Underneath the velvet sky,
I close my eyes and wonder why.
The stars ignite dreams yet to be,
The night's breath guides me, tenderly.

A Tapestry of Sleep Songs

Whispers weave through dusky air,
A tapestry beyond compare.
Each thread a tale of night's embrace,
In slumber's depths, we find our place.

Melodies drift like autumn leaves,
Carried gently by night's reprieves.
Every note, a feather's fall,
A sweet lull in the cosmic call.

In the dark, our dreams unite,
Stories spun in silken light.
With every hum, each soft refrain,
We dance through realms where love remains.

Rounded by voices, soft and warm,
Caught in the night, a tender swarm.
In this cradle, the heart belongs,
Wrapped forever in sleep songs.

Echoes of Togetherness

In the quiet of the night,
Whispers blend and dance.
Hearts beat in rhythm,
In this sacred trance.

Each laugh a gentle wave,
Trust woven with care.
Memories like soft threads,
Binding us, laid bare.

A touch, a knowing glance,
Journey shared as one.
Every moment cherished,
Until the night is done.

Through storms and through light,
We find our way again.
Together, hand in hand,
Love shall always reign.

Echoes of our voices,
Hang in the evening air.
A symphony of joy,
Forever we will share.

Soothing Starlit Tales

Under blankets of stars,
We weave tales so bright.
Each story a shimmer,
In the velvet night.

Whispers float like feathers,
On a gentle breeze.
Magic in the silence,
As the world finds ease.

Moonlight paints our dreams,
In shades of silver blue.
Every star a beacon,
Guiding me to you.

With every shared secret,
Our hearts learn to soar.
In this starlit wonder,
We discover more.

Soothing are the tales,
In these tranquil hours.
Boundless is the love,
That in silence flowers.

Softly Fade Away

In the dusk of the day,
Soft shadows creep in.
Colors blur and blend,
As sunlight grows thin.

Whispers of the evening,
Clutch at fading light.
Each heartbeat echoes,
In the softening night.

Dreams begin to wander,
On a fragile breeze.
Hope hangs like a promise,
Among the swaying trees.

Memories linger low,
In the golden haze.
Fleeting moments dance,
In soft, enchanted ways.

As the stars awaken,
Peace envelops all.
In the hush, we listen,
To the night's soft call.

Constellation of Calm

In the vast expanse,
Serenity gleams bright.
Stars whisper directions,
In the cloak of night.

Together we will wander,
Beneath skies so wide.
Each moment a treasure,
With you by my side.

Glimmers of the cosmos,
Wrap us in their grace.
Finding endless beauty,
In this sacred space.

With every heartbeat heard,
Peace unfurls its wings.
In the calm of the dark,
The universe sings.

As dreamers, we are lost,
In life's sweet embrace.
A constellation bright,
Our love finds its place.

Whispers Underneath the Stars

Beneath a canvas filled with light,
The whispers dance, a soft delight.
In shadows deep, our secrets twine,
As constellations start to shine.

The nightingale sings a tender song,
Where hearts entwine, where we belong.
With every sigh, the world feels right,
In whispers shared beneath the night.

The breeze carries tales of old,
Of lovers brave and dreams bold.
Each star a promise, burning bright,
Guides our souls through the twilight.

With every flutter, the silence breaks,
In laughter soft, the magic wakes.
We weave our hopes, our fears take flight,
In whispers shared beneath the night.

So let us linger, just you and I,
As moonlit journeys drift and sigh.
In celestial arms, we unite,
In whispers shared beneath the night.

Harmonies of the Night

The moonlight casts its silver sheen,
While shadows play, a gentle scene.
A symphony of stars aligns,
In harmony, our hearts entwine.

The cool night air sings soft refrains,
As whispers echo through the plains.
Each note a promise, bright and clear,
In harmonies, we draw you near.

A rustle of leaves, a call to roam,
In nature's arms, we find a home.
With every heartbeat, life unfolds,
In harmonies of dreams retold.

With fireflies sparking the darkened glade,
Our laughter dances, never fades.
In the stillness, joy ignites,
In harmonies of soft delights.

So let the night guide what we seek,
With melodies where spirits speak.
In cosmic chords, the world ignites,
In harmonies of starry nights.

Dreams Woven in Moonlight

In moonlit glades where shadows play,
Our dreams emerge, then drift away.
With every beam, the visions soar,
In magic spun forevermore.

The night enfolds us in its arms,
Protects our secrets, our quiet charms.
Each silver thread of light a sign,
In dreams woven, our souls align.

We chase the stars with hopeful hearts,
In whispered prayers, the journey starts.
Beneath the glow, we dare to trust,
In dreams woven, we find our must.

Each flicker bright, a pulse, a spark,
Guides our way through the deepest dark.
In every shimmer, love ignites,
In dreams woven on endless nights.

So linger close, let magic sway,
In moonlit silence, come what may.
We'll weave our wishes, twine them tight,
In dreams woven in the soft moonlight.

Synchronized Silhouettes

In twilight's glow, our shadows blend,
Two silhouettes that twist and bend.
With every step, the world must fade,
In synchronized dance, love is made.

The stars above, in silence gleam,
As we unfold, a tender dream.
Through whispered breezes, our hearts race,
In synchronized beats, we find our place.

We move as one, a graceful glide,
With every glance, we turn the tide.
In mirrored secrets, deep and bright,
In synchronized steps through the night.

A fleeting moment, time suspends,
In shadows cast, the magic bends.
With every twirl, a promise set,
In synchronized love, we won't forget.

So let us dance till morning's glow,
Through every high and every low.
In perfect time, our spirits light,
In synchronized motions of the night.

Restful Rhythms

In gentle waves, the night unfolds,
A soothing pulse, a story told.
The stars align, a calming light,
Embracing dreams that take to flight.

Silence speaks in whispered tones,
A lullaby that gently drones.
Each breath a note, a soft embrace,
Together drawn in time and space.

Moonlit shadows dance on ground,
While crickets play their nightly sound.
Nature's heart beats strong and true,
In restful rhythms, we renew.

With every sigh, the world slows down,
A tender peace, a borrowed crown.
In this stillness, we find our way,
To brighter hopes for a new day.

The night wraps all in velvet care,
As stars weave stories in the air.
In harmony, we find our grace,
In restful rhythms, we hold space.

Threads of Harmonic Tranquility

Within the weave of twilight's blend,
The threads of peace begin to send.
A gentle hand, a soft caress,
In harmony, we find our rest.

Dewdrops glisten in the light,
Each one a song, a memory bright.
In every breath, the silence sways,
A tapestry of soothing ways.

Through echoes of the whispering breeze,
The heart finds solace in the trees.
Each rustling leaf, a note in tune,
A serenade beneath the moon.

With every glance at starlit skies,
The soul awakens, learns to rise.
In threads of harmony, we find,
A tranquil space for heart and mind.

Embracing stillness, we reset,
In twilight's grip, we do not fret.
For every rhythm softly spun,
Threads unite us, one by one.

A Symphony of Nighttime Whispers

Underneath the moon's soft gaze,
A symphony begins to raise.
With every star, a note so clear,
A melody, we lend our ear.

The rustling winds, a gentle sigh,
Conceal the secrets passing by.
In twilight's arms, the shadows play,
As dreams unfold and drift away.

Each chirp and croon, a rhythmic chime,
In soothing tones, we lose our time.
A canvas dark, where sounds ignite,
Transforming stillness into light.

In whispered songs of nature's flow,
We find the strength that helps us grow.
A serenade, both bold and meek,
In nighttime's breath, it's peace we seek.

The echoes linger, soft and sweet,
A symphony beneath our feet.
With every note, we come alive,
In nighttime whispers, we arrive.

The Security of Silent Melodies

In quietude, we find our space,
A haven wrapped in night's embrace.
The world recedes, a distant hum,
In silent melodies, we come.

Each heartbeat dances, slow and soft,
As shadows cradle dreams aloft.
With every breath, we weave our ties,
Creating comfort, where love lies.

The night unveils a canvas deep,
Where whispers walk and secrets seep.
In peaceful tones, the heart beats strong,
In silent melodies, we belong.

No need for words, just gentle sighs,
For in this stillness, time complies.
The world may swirl, but we remain,
In security, we break the chain.

So let the hours softly blend,
Embracing silence, till the end.
For in the hush, our souls will find,
The security of love entwined.

Evenings in Harmony

The sun dips low, a soft embrace,
Colors swirl in a warm, bright space.
Whispers of night begin to play,
As daylight fades, it melts away.

Stars awaken, kind and bright,
Filling the canvas, a stunning sight.
Moonbeams dance on the gentle breeze,
Nature sighs in a surge of peace.

Crickets sing with a tranquil tune,
Under the gaze of a silver moon.
Night creatures stir from their hidden lairs,
While dreams unfold in secret layers.

Each moment lingers, a sacred spot,
A symphony played, with each soft thought.
We sit in stillness, hearts in tune,
As evening whispers, sweet as June.

The world slows down, a gentle sigh,
In the hush of night, we know not why.
Together we find a soothing balm,
In evenings wrapped in nature's calm.

Gentle Tides of Night

The moonlight spills on the water's face,
Ripples dance in a brisk embrace.
Stars reflect on a velvet sea,
Whispers carried from the breeze so free.

Gentle waves as they kiss the shore,
A melody sung forevermore.
Crickets chime, a rhythmic song,
In the quiet night, where we belong.

Seashell secrets, tales of old,
Laughter echoing, brave and bold.
Under the sky, vast and divine,
Each heartbeat echoes, a signal sign.

The night unfolds its mystery,
Wrapped in the warmth of history.
Tides of dreams begin to swell,
A story told, a sacred spell.

With each tide that ebbs and flows,
The heart remembers, the spirit knows.
In gentle rhythms, we find our place,
Embraced by night's soft, loving grace.

The Reach of Dusk's Caress

A canvas painted in shades of gold,
The horizon whispers the tales of old.
Dusk approaches on silent feet,
As shadows lengthen, the night's heartbeat.

Amber hues blend into twilight's glow,
Softly the stars begin to show.
Silence blankets the waking earth,
In dusk's embrace, we find our mirth.

Birds take flight on the evening air,
A fleeting glimpse, a moment rare.
Branches sway in a gentle ballet,
Inviting peace, come what may.

Wisps of cloud in a lavender sky,
Drawn together like a lullaby.
Nature hums in a soothing tone,
In dusk's caress, we're not alone.

With the night's arrival, dreams take flight,
Drawing us deeper into the night.
Wrapped in warmth, under stars we lay,
As dusk's embrace guides the end of day.

Treetop Whispers

In the forest where the wild winds sigh,
Treetops sway against the open sky.
Leaves are moving in a gentle dance,
While nature calls in a sweet romance.

Branches rustle, secrets shared,
Stories of life, joys declared.
Beneath the canopy, shadows play,
Filling the heart with warmth and sway.

Sunbeams filter through the green,
Dancing down where we've seldom been.
Amidst the whisper, calm and deep,
In the treetop silence, our souls leap.

Each creak and groan tells time's old tale,
As nature's breath weaves the softest veil.
With every moment, a chance to grow,
In the embrace of the leaves' soft flow.

In this realm of whispers and light,
Hearts find solace in the fading light.
Treetop dreams, where the wild things roam,
We carve our path and feel at home.

Embraced in Night's Lull

The stars above quietly glow,
In velvet skies where soft winds blow.
Each whisper holds a tender grace,
As shadows dance in night's embrace.

The moonlight bathes the world in peace,
While all the sounds of day do cease.
A melody of dreams unfurls,
As slumber weaves its magic pearls.

Crickets sing their lullabies,
While gentle breezes sigh and rise.
The night, a cradle, rocks so sweet,
Where weary souls can rest their feet.

In deep repose, the heart takes flight,
Embraced within the arms of night.
A tranquil world, both vast and wide,
Where joy and sorrow softly bide.

Resonances of Quietude

In the stillness, echoes play,
A gentle hush that drifts away.
Upon the breeze, soft secrets glide,
In peaceful realms where dreams abide.

The world slows down, a whispered tune,
Beneath the silver glow of moon.
Each heartbeat finds its subtle blend,
In quietude, beginnings mend.

Like rustling leaves or flowing streams,
The silence wraps us in our dreams.
A canvas stretched where thoughts entwine,
In resonances so pure, divine.

Time stands still, a sacred space,
Where echoes leave their tender trace.
In calmness, we uncover light,
Together, lost in endless night.

Dreamwoven Whispers

In the twilight's gentle weave,
Dreams take form; they interleave.
With every sigh, the heart takes flight,
In whispers borne of soft delight.

Each thought a thread, so brightly spun,
We weave our hopes till night is done.
Through veils of sleep, the visions call,
In quiet realms where shadows fall.

Stars cascade like silver rain,
They trace the paths where dreams remain.
While night unfolds its mystic art,
These dreamwoven whispers touch the heart.

A tapestry of twilight's glow,
Each spark a tale, a seed to sow.
In slumber's dance, our spirits soar,
As whispers guide us evermore.

The Journey to Dreamland

Beneath the starlit sky we roam,
In search of dreams, we find our home.
With every step, the shadows play,
A guide to where our spirits sway.

Through fragrant fields of midnight bloom,
Our hearts alight dispel the gloom.
Each whispered wish a feathered flight,
Across the canvas of the night.

In twilight's arms, we lose our cares,
As magic lingers in the airs.
The journey calls through silent lands,
Embraced by night's compassionate hands.

With every heartbeat, dreams unfold,
In whispered tales of love retold.
The journey to dreamland's grace,
Awaits us in this cherished space.

Timeworn Nightwhispers

In shadows deep, the secrets sigh,
Old tales rise where daylight dies.
Moonlit whispers through the trees,
Echo softly, carried by the breeze.

Ancient stars blink in the night,
Guiding dreams, a distant light.
Hearts entwined in silence weave,
Timeworn echoes never leave.

Stars above, a watchful gaze,
Wrapping whispers in a haze.
Each breath holds a world apart,
Night's embrace, a tender heart.

Where time stands still, presence near,
In memory's song, we share our fear.
Through the veils of twilight's grace,
Timeworn night, a sacred place.

Beneath the moon, shadows dance,
Every glance, a fleeting chance.
With every sigh, we drift and flow,
In night's embrace, our spirits grow.

Sweet Refrains of Comfort

In gentle waves, the music plays,
Softening the edges of the days.
Faintly humming, a lullaby,
Sweet refrains that never die.

Through open windows, breezes flow,
Carrying murmurs, warm and slow.
Each note a soft hand to hold,
Woven tales of warmth retold.

Gentle laughter fills the air,
Wrapping loved ones in its care.
Moments captured, timeless grace,
In sweet refrain, we find our place.

Softly spoken, whispered truth,
Reminds us always of our youth.
Comfort finds us, night and day,
With sweet refrains to light the way.

As shadows stretch, the melody,
Flows like rivers, pure and free.
Hearts embrace the sound of bliss,
In sweet refrains, we find our kiss.

Voices in the Dark

Whispers echo, soft and clear,
Voices in the dark, we hear.
Secrets linger, tales unfold,
Stories lost, yet never old.

Beneath the hush of moonlit skies,
A symphony of silent cries.
Every shadow holds a name,
In stillness, passion ignites the flame.

Carried on the evening breeze,
Voices tangled in the trees.
Living memories intertwine,
In the dark, our souls align.

Through quiet nights, we venture deep,
To find the dreams that softly sleep.
In whispered tones, we weave our fate,
With voices guiding, never late.

Oh, to hear the distant call,
Of those who rise, and those who fall.
Voices linger, shadows play,
In the dark, we find our way.

Lull in the Night

When dusk descends and stars appear,
A lull in the night invites us near.
Softly sighing, the world does rest,
Finding solace, we are blessed.

Gentle dreams begin to weave,
In the stillness, hearts believe.
Time slows down, a tender pause,
Wrapped in night's calming laws.

Moonbeams dance on silver streams,
Cradling hopes and whispered dreams.
Every heartbeat sings in tune,
Beneath the watchful eye of moon.

Stars converse in quiet light,
Sowing peace throughout the night.
Every breath, a soft embrace,
In the lull, we find our place.

As slumber falls and shadows fade,
In night's embrace, we are remade.
A lull in the night, pure delight,
Carving calm in the endless flight.

Serenades in Silence

Whispers dance on feathered wings,
In the quietude, the night sings.
Stars shimmer softly, a gentle glow,
Dreams awaken, as breezes flow.

Moonlight bathes the world in peace,
In this stillness, worries cease.
Hearts entwined in sacred space,
Time slows down, a sweet embrace.

Every sigh, a note in tune,
Under the watchful eye of the moon.
Echoes linger, secrets shared,
In this moment, souls bared.

Serenades in waltz-like flight,
In shadows deep, hearts feel light.
The silence wraps us, warm and kind,
In the harmony, love is blind.

Together we weave our melodious dream,
In silence profound, we become a team.
With each heartbeat, a love song grows,
In the serenade, true emotion flows.

Fluttering Hearts in Twilight

The dusk unveils its painted skies,
As day retreats, a soft reprise.
Fluttering hearts in twilight's embrace,
Love unravels at a gentle pace.

Beneath the blush of fading light,
We dance together, holding tight.
Whispers threaded like tender vines,
In this moment, the world aligns.

Stars awaken, one by one,
The canvas darkens, the magic spun.
Soft breezes carry secrets near,
In twilight's hush, there's nothing to fear.

Time stands still, in this lull,
With every heartbeat, the night is full.
Fluttering hearts, a sweet refrain,
In the twilight, love's voice remains.

As shadows whisper, dreams take flight,
Together we bask in fading light.
Two souls intertwined under the sky,
Fluttering hearts, forever fly.

Constellations of Harmony

In the tapestry of the night,
Constellations gleam, pure delight.
Each star a story, a tale untold,
In their brightness, dreams unfold.

Guided by the celestial dance,
In their glow, we find our chance.
Harmony wrapped in starlit grace,
In this silence, we find our place.

Like whispers woven through the dark,
Each moment ignites a spark.
Connected through these cosmic streams,
In the night, we share our dreams.

With every glance, the universe sighs,
Boundless beauty in cosmic ties.
Constellations of love align,
In the vastness, your heart is mine.

Together we wander, hand in hand,
Lost in the magic of a starry land.
In harmony, our spirits soar,
In constellations, forevermore.

Gentle Rhythms of Us

The world sways in gentle tune,
Underneath the silver moon.
Heartbeat dances, soft and slow,
In the rhythm, love we sow.

Every touch, a wave's caress,
In our silence, we find bliss.
Gentle whispers fill the air,
In this moment, we are rare.

Seasons turn, yet we remain,
In every joy, in every pain.
With every heartbeat, a pulse of trust,
In the gentle rhythms, love's a must.

Together we weave a tender song,
In the melody, we both belong.
Through years and changes, hand in hand,
In the rhythms, we understand.

Echoes linger, soft and clear,
In our hearts, love's symphony dear.
With gentle rhythms, spirits thrive,
In this dance, we are alive.

Cradled in Melodic Dreams

In twilight's hush, the stars alight,
Whispers of night take gentle flight.
Softly cradled, in shadows deep,
We drift away on waves of sleep.

Moonbeams dance on silken sheets,
Melodies weave through starlit streets.
Every note a tender sigh,
Guiding dreams where wishes lie.

The lullabies of softest night,
Wrap the world in pure delight.
In waking hours, we'll long for this,
The soft embrace of night's sweet kiss.

With every breath, the dreams unfold,
Stories in silver, wrapped in gold.
Cradled close in sounds so sweet,
Hearts entwined, our souls complete.

As dawn approaches, the dreams will fade,
Yet in our hearts, they will cascade.
Forever danced in twilight's gleam,
We'll cherish nights of melodic dreams.

A Tapestry of Sleep Sounds

Threads of night weave silent grace,
Crickets sing in a soft embrace.
A tapestry of whispers spun,
Where dreams begin and hearts are won.

The wind carries secrets untold,
Through branches bending, through leaves that fold.
A melody of night includes
The murmur of distant solitude.

Pillow clouds cradle weary heads,
In gentle beds where comfort spreads.
Each sound a brush, a stroke so light,
Painting calm upon the night.

In this realm where slumber reigns,
Peace unfurls in quiet chains.
A tapestry of sleep surrounds,
In the beauty of these soothing sounds.

As dreams take flight in softest air,
We find the solace lingering there.
In the fabric of night, we find our peace,
And in the dawn, it will not cease.

Night's Tender Embrace

In the stillness, shadows play,
Night wraps the world in soft array.
With gentle arms, it pulls us near,
Night's tender embrace calms all fear.

Stars twinkle like eyes from above,
Whispering secrets, a promise of love.
The moon sings sweetly, a lullaby,
Filling the night as dreams float by.

Beneath a sky of velvet hue,
We breathe in peace, the night feels new.
Every heartbeat, a soothing sound,
In night's embrace, true joy is found.

The world outside may fade away,
In this sacred space, forever stay.
Hold onto the warmth, let worries cease,
Cradled softly in night's release.

As dawn peeks through with golden light,
We'll carry forth the whispers of night.
But in our hearts, where magic stays,
Lives the comfort of night's gentle ways.

The Symphony of Kindred Spirits

In twilight's glow, our spirits blend,
A symphony that has no end.
Kindred hearts in harmony,
Dancing beneath the ancient tree.

Each note we share, a sacred bond,
Echoes of dreams that we respond.
With laughter bright and whispers low,
Our song weaves threads that brightly glow.

Underneath the watchful stars,
We find our truth, we heal our scars.
In silence deep, where souls unite,
A symphony sings through the night.

Together we rise, together we fall,
In every heartbeat, we hear the call.
With every sigh, with every glance,
Life's melody gives us a chance.

As dawn breaks forth with a golden hue,
We carry the music, pure and true.
Forever bound by this sweet choir,
The symphony of hearts' desire.

Harmonies of the Heart

In whispers soft, our stories blend,
A melody that knows no end.
Each note a treasure, held so dear,
In this sweet song, you're always near.

With every sigh, a rhythm flows,
A dance of love, where passion grows.
The heartbeat sways in twilight's glow,
Together still, through highs and lows.

In silence, there, our spirits soar,
A brush of hands, a gentle roar.
The world fades out, we find our place,
In harmonies, we leave a trace.

Through laughter's light and sorrow's shade,
In every chord, our souls displayed.
The music binds, with threads unseen,
A tapestry of what has been.

In every tune, our truth unfolds,
A secret language, one that holds.
With every strum, our hearts ignite,
In endless song, we find the light.

Twilight Serenades

As daylight dims, the stars appear,
The night unfolds, so calm and clear.
A serenade of crickets starts,
Echoing soft in dreamy hearts.

Whispers brush against the air,
A symphony of love to share.
In twilight's arms, we sway and sing,
Joyful notes the night will bring.

With every breath, a story told,
In shadows deep, our dreams unfold.
The moonlight dances on our skin,
A serenade, where love begins.

With silver threads, the night weaves tight,
In gentle tones, we find our light.
As midnight calls, we hold on close,
In whispered songs, we make a toast.

In twilight's glow, our voices blend,
A melody that knows no end.
As stars align, we find our way,
In twilight's serenade, we stay.

The Comfort of Gentle Tones

In softest whispers, comfort found,
A lullaby in love's surround.
Each word a brush, a tender stroke,
In gentle tones, our hearts awoke.

With every touch, a soothing plea,
Together lost, just you and me.
A tranquil space, where worries cease,
In mellow notes, we find our peace.

The warmth of hands, the hush of night,
In every glance, a pure delight.
The gentle flow of time stands still,
In harmony, we feel the thrill.

With every sigh, the moments soar,
In soft embrace, we yearn for more.
A symphony of hearts entwined,
In tender tones, love's song defined.

As echoes fade, we hold the calm,
In soothing waves, we share a balm.
With every note, our spirits rise,
In gentle tones, we find the skies.

Stars in Our Voices

Each word we speak, a star ignites,
A shining dream in quiet nights.
Together crafting tales divine,
In every echo, you are mine.

With laughter bright, we paint the skies,
In whispered hopes, our spirits rise.
The universe can hear our song,
A melody that feels so strong.

Through silver nights, our voices blend,
A cosmic dance that knows no end.
We journey far, yet stay in tune,
With starlit paths beneath the moon.

As shadows play, we sing along,
In every heart, a perfect song.
With every line, the night awakes,
A harmony that love creates.

In constellations, we find our light,
With stars in voices, shining bright.
Together here, forever free,
In this sweet song, just you and me.

Distant Echoes

In valleys deep, a sound takes flight,
A memory lost, in fading light.
Faint whispers call from afar,
Ghostly tales beneath the star.

Footsteps tread on ancient ground,
Where silence reigns, no voice is found.
Yet in the breeze, a song we hear,
The past resounds, forever near.

Echoes dance on winds so free,
Filling hearts with mystery.
Time's embrace both warm and cold,
In distant dreams, our stories told.

Arriving soft, like shadows cast,
The echoes linger, hold us fast.
In twilight's glow, they leave their trace,
Reminders sweet of time's embrace.

Close Hearts

In gentle breaths, our secrets shared,
A bond that's strong, forever dared.
With every laugh, the world grows bright,
In your embrace, all feels just right.

Eyes that meet, a silent pact,
In every glance, there's no need to act.
Together we rise, side by side,
In this life, our hearts collide.

Through storms we walk, hand in hand,
In every challenge, we take a stand.
With love as our guiding star,
We'll find home, no matter how far.

In whispered dreams that softly glow,
Our journey flows, like rivers slow.
Close hearts entwined, forever true,
In sacred moments created by two.

Celestial Comforts

Stars blanketed in velvet skies,
Each twinkle tells the tales of sighs.
With moonlit paths, our spirits soar,
In the cosmos, we find much more.

Galaxies spin, a dance so divine,
In their embrace, our souls align.
The night whispers secrets in the air,
A cosmic tale beyond compare.

Nebulae glow, colors bright,
Painting dreams in endless night.
With every gaze, we feel the pull,
The universe knows the heart is full.

In gentle warmth, the stardust we trace,
Each heartbeat finds a special place.
Celestial comforts, vast and wide,
In the heavens, our hopes abide.

The Language of Softness

In tender words, our hearts will speak,
A gentle touch when moments peak.
The quiet sighs, an artless grace,
In softness found, we find our place.

Whispers linger, a soothing balm,
In this embrace, the world turns calm.
With every glance, affection grows,
In silent stories, the heart knows.

The warmth of hands, so close and dear,
In every heartbeat, love draws near.
Where words may fail, our souls ignite,
In the language of softness, hearts take flight.

Tenderness wrapped in twilight's hum,
A symphony where dreams can come.
Each moment shared, a sacred thread,
In the language of softness, love is bred.

Whispers of the Night

As shadows creep, the world grows still,
Nighttime whispers, soft and chill.
The stars above, they blink and sigh,
While secrets dance in the velvet sky.

The moon's bright face, a guiding light,
Illuminates paths through the night.
In quiet corners, stories unfold,
In whispered dreams, our hearts are bold.

The breeze carries tales we share,
In tranquil moments, love laid bare.
Each heartbeat echoes in the dark,
With every sigh, we leave our mark.

In the hush of night, we find our truth,
The whispers speak of eternal youth.
In serene spaces where shadows play,
The whispers of the night guide our way.

Swaying to Sleep

Night whispers soft and clear,
The world fades into dreams,
Cradled in a lullaby,
Resting where the silence gleams.

Gentle shadows dance around,
While stars twinkle from afar,
Wrapped in warmth, the heart now pounds,
Beneath the watchful star.

Tucked in close, the worries wane,
The breeze sings through the trees,
With every breath, we drift away,
In moments like these, we're free.

Whispers blend with fading light,
As night unfolds its velvet sheet,
Swaying slowly, holding tight,
To dreams where souls shall meet.

In slumber's grip, we find our peace,
Each sigh, a soothing balm,
With every heartbeat, troubles cease,
In sleep's embrace, we're calm.

Melodies We Weave

Notes of laughter fill the air,
With every chord, a story starts,
Through the echoes, hearts declare,
The symphony of loving hearts.

Threads of joy entwined in sound,
Harmonies that softly glow,
In every note, a love profound,
Together, watch our passions flow.

With each strum, the world ignites,
As music paints our skies anew,
Dancing shadows, twinkling lights,
In every verse, our souls pursue.

Together we create a dream,
As melodies weave through the night,
In the rhythm, we find the theme,
Of love that makes our spirits light.

In this dance, we find our place,
Where melodies are spun and played,
In the silence, we leave a trace,
Of every song that's serenade.

Choruses Under Starlight

Underneath a velvet sky,
We gather 'round and sing,
Voices rising, hearts in tune,
As night invites the spring.

Stars are shimmering far above,
Casting dreams in gentle glow,
In every chorus, whispers love,
As time begins to slow.

Fingers strumming, soft and slow,
With every note, we dare to dream,
In the magic, spirits grow,
Together, we're a gleaming team.

Beneath the heavens, tangled light,
We weave our stories, soft yet bright,
In harmony, our souls unite,
With every breath, we take to flight.

As night deepens, we will share,
Secrets only stars can hear,
Together always, free as air,
With every chorus, drawing near.

The Calm We Hold

In the quiet of the dawn,
Where whispers blend with sunlight,
We find a peace to lean upon,
Chasing away the night.

Gentle waves of morning hue,
Invite our hearts to breathe,
In every pause, a moment new,
Together, we shall weave.

With every thought, we softly sow,
Seeds of stillness in our mind,
Finding rhythm, letting go,
As the calm begins to bind.

Holding close the warmth of now,
In blissful breath, we find the way,
With every heartbeat, we allow,
The beauty of a brand new day.

In this space where we belong,
Time unfolds like petals wide,
In every sigh, a soothing song,
Together, let love be our guide.

Harmonies Beneath the Skies

Whispers of the evening breeze,
Notes that dance between the trees,
Stars above begin to shine,
Hearts around intertwine.

Crickets sing their ancient tune,
Beneath the watchful, silver moon,
Melodies of night unfold,
Stories whispered, never told.

Gentle waves upon the shore,
Carry tales of those before,
Each soft sigh, a sweet embrace,
Nature's music, time and space.

Clouds that drift, so soft and light,
Painting shadows in the night,
Harmony's sweet lullaby,
Echoes of a fleeting sigh.

Underneath the vast expanse,
Souls awakened in a dance,
Carried forth by cosmic winds,
To where every journey begins.

Moments in Moonlit Silence

The silver sheen on silent lakes,
A world at rest, as stillness wakes,
Reflections deep in tranquil night,
Whispers carried with soft light.

Footsteps soft upon the ground,
In this peace, no other sound,
Just the pulse of time's gentle flow,
As dreams begin to softly grow.

The moonlight bathes the world so bright,
Guides our hearts through silent night,
Each breath taken, a quiet pause,
Nature's song, a sacred cause.

Stars hang low, a jeweled thread,
Woven paths where footsteps led,
In this moment, we unite,
Lost in depths of purest light.

Time stands still in this embrace,
Our spirits find their sacred space,
In moonlit silence, we belong,
A symphony, a timeless song.

Tuning into Tranquility

In the quiet of the dawn,
Gentle light just softly drawn,
Birds awaken with a cheer,
Nature's whispers drawing near.

The world hums a soothing tune,
As warmth replaces cool of moon,
Each note a breath, a calming breeze,
Time slows down, invites us to ease.

Through the fields of emerald green,
In every glance, a world unseen,
Footsteps soft on dew-kissed grass,
Moments linger, slow to pass.

Clouds drift softly, dreams unspun,
Underneath the rising sun,
Harmony in every sigh,
Life unfolds as we comply.

Embrace the calm, let worries fade,
In tranquility, serenade,
With open hearts, we find our way,
In this peace, forever stay.

Twilit Voices

Beneath the fading light we stand,
Whispers of the night command.
Softly weave the twilight's thread,
In the hush where dreams are bred.

Stars begin their gentle wake,
Fragrant night, the world will take.
Echoes dance on summer air,
Secrets sung, with tender care.

Flickering shadows rise and sway,
Carrying our hopes away.
With each sigh, the night begins,
Dancing where the light thins.

In the stillness, hearts so true,
Knowing all we've shared anew.
Listening close, the world seems light,
As twilit voices kiss the night.

With the moon as our only guide,
In this moment, we abide.
Together in this sacred space,
Whispers form an ever trace.

Dream Songs of Togetherness

In the hush between the songs,
Where our hearts have always belonged.
Melodies of the softest tune,
Underneath the watchful moon.

Footsteps echo, softly trace,
Memories in a warm embrace.
Boundless dreams on gentle wings,
Awakened by the joy it brings.

Every heartbeat sings of us,
In the starlight, we place our trust.
Each note lingers, whispers sweet,
Together, we find our heartbeat.

With the dawn, new dreams arise,
Coloring the endless skies.
Hand in hand, we'll face the day,
In this dance, we find our way.

In every breath, a song we find,
The warmth of love, forever kind.
Dream songs carry us above,
In this realm of endless love.

Slumbering Echoes

In the quiet of the night,
Slumbering echoes take their flight.
Waves of peace begin to sweep,
Lulls the world to gentle sleep.

Stars reflect on tranquil seas,
Singing softly through the trees.
In the stillness, hearts unite,
Cradled by the silver light.

Whispers woven, faint and low,
Guide our dreams where visions flow.
While shadows play in silent grace,
Embracing time in this dear place.

Every sigh, a story told,
Of sacred bonds that will not fold.
As night enfolds us in its care,
Slumbering echoes linger there.

With dawn's light, we shall awake,
But these dreams, we shall not shake.
For in the night, our souls take flight,
Together in the soft moonlight.

Shadows Sing Softly

When shadows start to softly sway,
Nighttime wraps the world in gray.
Silent echoes fill the air,
Carried gently, everywhere.

In the twilight, whispers gleam,
Painting softly every dream.
Moonlit paths, a silver hue,
Shadows dance for me and you.

With every sigh, the night's embrace,
Holds the warmth of this dear place.
Voices blend in perfect tune,
Beneath the watchful eyes of moon.

As the stars begin to gleam,
We ignite the wishful dream.
In this moment, spirits soar,
When shadows sing, we long for more.

Together, we shall face the dawn,
With whispered dreams that linger on.
In the silence, love takes flight,
As shadows sing soft through the night.

Heartstrings in Twilight

The sun dips low, a whispering glow,
Casting shadows where dreams softly flow.
In twilight's embrace, secrets unfold,
Memories dance, their stories retold.

Soft sighs linger, a sweet, tender breath,
In the hush of dusk, we flirt with death.
Hearts interlace beneath starlit skies,
A tapestry woven from silent goodbyes.

The moon, a sentinel, watches in grace,
Illuminating paths that time can't erase.
Fingertips brush, a connection so deep,
Cradling moments we promise to keep.

As night wraps around, we hold onto fate,
Each heartbeat echoes, refusing to wait.
In this fleeting hour, love's magic is true,
Heartstrings entwined, just me and you.

Whispers of longing fill the cool night air,
With every pulse, I find you are there.
In twilight's arms, our souls find their song,
Together we linger, where we both belong.

Nights Filled with Nostalgia

Beneath the stars, where memories glow,
Nights filled with laughter, echoes of old.
Stories unfold in the soft candlelight,
As shadows entwine, we cherish the night.

The clock softly ticks, yet time stands still,
Recalling the moments that gave us a thrill.
Photographs linger in the corners of mind,
Capturing laughter we struggle to find.

In rhythmic whispers, the past calls our names,
A dance of remembrance, igniting old flames.
Underneath the canopy, wrapped in warm bliss,
Each breath is a memory, each sigh, a kiss.

We wander through dreams that once felt so real,
Tracing the pathways our hearts used to feel.
In the moon's gentle light, reflections collide,
Together we journey, with time as our guide.

As night drifts away, leaving shadows of light,
We savor the whispers of love's sweet delight.
In these quiet moments, forever we'll blend,
A tapestry woven, where love has no end.

The Caress of Gentle Harmonies

Notes drift like petals on a soft summer breeze,
Whispered serenades wrapped in melodies.
Each chord a treasure, each song a delight,
As the heart sways gently through the velvet night.

In the stillness, sound paints colors so bright,
Harmonies linger, banishing fright.
The warmth of the strings, soft whispers ignite,
As the soul sways under the starlight's light.

With every vibration, a memory awakes,
Soft shadows dance as the moonlight breaks.
Gentle harmonies cradle the night,
Healing the wounds that once felt so tight.

The caress of music, a balm for the soul,
Filling the spaces that once felt so whole.
Each note a promise, a dream to bestow,
In the silence that follows, our hearts overflow.

As dawn starts to break, the lullabies fade,
Yet the echoes of love in our hearts are made.
In the symphony's wake, we softly will sway,
Guided by music, we'll find our own way.

Warmth of Evening Tales

The sun descends, draping the earth in gold,
Evening whispers secrets, both gentle and bold.
Around the fire, stories weave and entwine,
Illuminated faces, the warmth of the brine.

With each shared tale, laughter fills the air,
Memories linger, beckoning us to care.
Voices rise like embers, dancing in the night,
In this circle of love, everything feels right.

Tales of the past blend with dreams yet to come,
Where every heartbeat feels like a drum.
In the soft glow, our spirits unite,
Wrapped in the magic of this tranquil night.

The warmth of the tales wraps us like a shawl,
Each story a jewel, a treasure for all.
We capture the fleeting, the moments so rare,
In the hearth of our hearts, with love laid bare.

As stars twinkle brightly, the night whispers low,
In the warmth of these tales, our love will forever grow.
With each flickering flame, we share and create,
A bond made of stories that time can't abate.

Together We Drift

Together we drift on a gentle tide,
With whispers of waves, our hearts glide.
The sun paints the sky in hues of gold,
In this moment, our stories unfold.

Hand in hand, we chase the light,
Beneath the stars, our dreams take flight.
In every laugh, in every sigh,
We find the reason, you and I.

The world fades away, just us in the sea,
Where time suspends, we're wild and free.
A journey uncharted, hearts so bold,
Together we drift, our tales retold.

With every wave, a new secret's shared,
In silence, the moments, we've always dared.
As twilight beckons, shadows play,
Forever and always, we'll find our way.

So here we remain, lost in the flow,
In the heart of the ocean, love continues to grow.
Together we drift, beneath the stars' glow,
A bond unbreakable, where dreams overflow.

Songs of the Quiet

In the stillness, soft notes rise,
They dance upon the night, like fireflies.
Whispers of nature, a gentle hum,
In the heart of the quiet, we become.

The rustling leaves share tales untold,
While the moon glimmers with silvery gold.
Each breath a melody, pure and sweet,
In this tranquil moment, our souls meet.

Echoes of laughter from distant past,
In the songs of the quiet, memories cast.
The world may bustle, but here we find,
A soft serenade that soothes the mind.

Beneath the stars, we close our eyes,
Where the quiet speaks and the heart flies.
In the realm of silence, hope ignites,
Creating magic in the starlit nights.

So let us linger, where stillness calls,
In the arms of the quiet, love enthralls.
A song of the night, as dreams take flight,
In the serene embrace, everything feels right.

Embracing the Night

In the hush of dusk, shadows creep,
Where the stars awake, and dreamers sleep.
Veils of twilight wrap us tight,
Together we stand, embracing the night.

With whispers of wind, secrets unfold,
In the tapestry of darkness, stories told.
Each twinkle above, a promise bright,
Illuminates paths in the soft moonlight.

The air is thick with serene delight,
As we wander through the enchanting sight.
Every heartbeat echoes, soft and slow,
In the timeless rhythm, together we flow.

Wrapped in the arms of the endless sky,
With every sigh, we learn to fly.
In the quiet, our spirits ignite,
With hope and dreams, embracing the night.

So take my hand, let's drift away,
To where stars sing, and shadows play.
In this sacred hour, everything feels right,
Together forever, embracing the night.

Serenade for Dreams

In the quiet hour, when shadows fall,
A serenade whispers, a sweet call.
Melodies drift through the midnight air,
Inviting our hearts to wander somewhere.

With soft lullabies from the moonlit sky,
We dream of the places where fantasies lie.
Each note, a flutter, a sigh of the soul,
In the warmth of the night, we feel whole.

The stars paint a canvas, so vast above,
A symphony woven with threads of love.
In this enchanting dance, we lose our way,
To the serenade that night has to say.

With every heartbeat, the dreams align,
In the embrace of the night, our spirits shine.
So let the music guide us, soft and sweet,
In the serenade for dreams, our souls meet.

As dawn approaches, the curtains of gold,
The echo of dreams, forever retold.
With the promise of morning, we'll rise and beam,
Carrying forth this serenade of dreams.

9 781805 605027